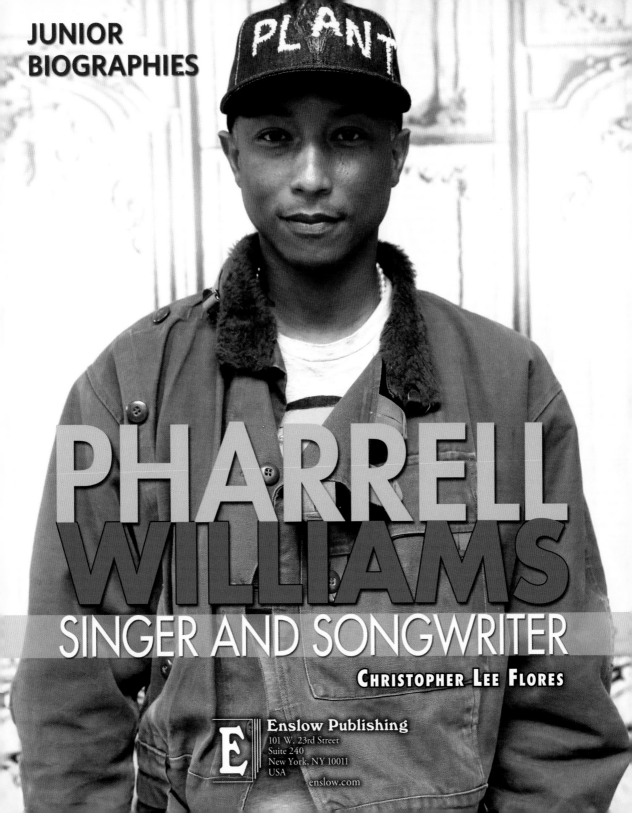

JUNIOR
BIOGRAPHIES

PHARRELL WILLIAMS
SINGER AND SONGWRITER

CHRISTOPHER LEE FLORES

Enslow Publishing
101 W. 23rd Street
Suite 240
New York, NY 10011
USA
enslow.com

album A collection of songs by one artist.

collaborator Someone who works with another person to create something.

contestant Someone who is part of a competition.

label A place that markets musicians to the public and helps to produce their music.

producer The person in charge of making a piece of art.

sound track A collection of music used in a movie.

studio A place where an artist works.

CONTENTS

CHAPTER 1

There's Nothing Wrong with Being a N.E.R.D

Pharrell Williams is a world-famous singer, rapper, and record **producer**. He is a Grammy Award winner and is known as an essential part of the music industry. The work that he and his team create will forever be a part of music history.

Pharrell Lanscilo Williams was born on April 5, 1973, in Virginia Beach, Virginia. His father, Pharoah, was a handyman; and his mother, Carolyn, was a teacher. He has two younger brothers: Cato and Psolomon Williams. His family was not a very musical one, but he played and sang along to records on a stereo with one of his aunts. As a kid in school, he was also known for tapping on his desk in order to create different rhythms and beats. He always enjoyed music, and his parents encouraged him to persue an education in his passion. But they didn't know how deep that passion would grow.

Pharrell Says:
"I lived in Normalville USA and I didn't look like the average kid."

A FRIENDSHIP AND A PASSION

Pharrell was in the seventh grade when he went to a summer band camp, where he played the keyboard and drums. It was there that he met Chad Hugo, who would become a lifelong friend and **collaborator**. Chad played the saxophone. They became very close at the camp and remained in touch, although they attended different schools. Pharrell attended Princess Anne High School, where he became a part of their marching

Located on the Atlantic Ocean, Virginia Beach is the most populated city in Virginia. Its most popular attraction is the beachfront.

band. Pharrell also loved to skateboard. Because of this, his friends gave him the nickname Skateboard P. He felt different and didn't think he fit in with the popular kids.

FUN FACT
Your heartbeat mimics the beat of the music you're listening to.

Chad Hugo and Pharrell began collaborating and creating music together before they were teenagers.

CHAPTER 2
A DISCOVERY OF N.E.R.D.s

In the early 1990s, Pharrell and Chad put together an R&B (rhythmn and blues) group. They called themselves the Neptunes. Also in the group were their friends Shay Haley and Mike Etheridge. They entered a high school talent show. In the audience sat a Grammy Award–winning record producer named Edward Theodore Riley, also known as Teddy Riley. His **studio** was near Princess Anne High School. When Riley heard the Neptunes, he signed them to his record **label**. But before they could become full-time musicians, they had to graduate high school.

THE NEPTUNES

The Neptunes got their start by producing music. While working with Riley, Pharrell took on some solo projects. In 1992, he wrote a verse for song for a group called Wreckx-N-Effects, which was #2 on the *Billboard* Hot 100 chart. Pharrell and Chad were a strong team and

slowly began to make a name for themselves. They worked with many different types of artists. Their sound changed as they experimented with different styles.

They worked on N.O.R.E's song "Superthug" in 1998, which reached #36 on the *Billboard* Hot 100. The popularity of the song made people curious about who was creating such

Producer Teddy Riley has worked with many famous artists, including Michael Jackson, Snoop Dogg, Usher, and Lady Gaga, as well as the boys from the Neptunes.

outstanding beats. They first gained commercial success working with the legendary Jay Z. Other artists they worked with include Kelis, Justin Timberlake, Snoop Dogg, Robin Thicke, Mariah Carey, and Nelly. With the evolution of their sound, the Neptunes were able to work across all genres of music.

Their first worldwide hit came in 2001 when they worked with Britney Spears on "I'm a Slave 4 U." Not only did they

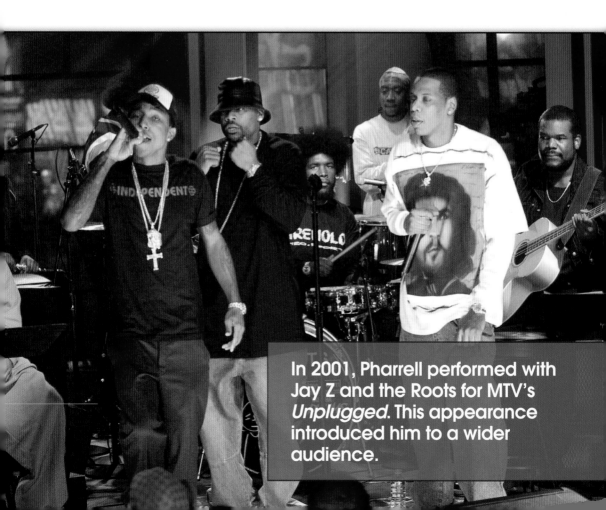

In 2001, Pharrell performed with Jay Z and the Roots for MTV's *Unplugged.* This appearance introduced him to a wider audience.

reach #1 in the United States, but they also reached #1 in several countries in Europe and South America.

In 2003, the Neptunes released an **album** called *The Neptunes Present…Clones.* It was a mix of original and remixed songs. The album went on to top the US *Billboard* 200 Albums chart. A year later, the Neptunes won two Grammy Awards, one of the music industry's highest honors. They won for both "Producer of the Year, Non-classical" and "Best Pop Vocal Album" for their work with Justin Timberlake.

N.E.R.D.

In 1999, Pharrell and Chad began another band. They called this side project N.E.R.D. (for **N**o one **E**ver **R**eally **D**ies). Their sound was a mix of rock, funk, pop, and hip-hop. Together, the group released four albums: *In Search of…, Fly or Die, Seeing Sounds,* and *Nothing.*

FUN FACTS
A song that gets stuck in your head on repeat is called an "ear worm."

Pharrell Says:

"We want to make music that reflected that. So people can look back twenty years from now and say, 'this is what was going on.' "

Their goal was to try to sound different from anything they had done before. One way of doing this was using live instruments as opposed to digital sounds. Their first album was not very successful, but their second album reached #6 on the *Billboard* 200 chart.

After they released their third album, they began touring. While on tour, they worked with new artists such as Kanye West, Rihanna, Lupe Fiasco, and Lincoln Park. One of their songs, "Soldier," which featured artists Santigold and Lil' Wayne, was put on the **sound track** for a re-invention of the teen drama *90210*.

With their fourth album, N.E.R.D. wanted to reflect the difficult times in the country. It was released in 2010, when the economy was bad and the United States was at war in the Middle East. They wanted to create an album that showed there was still beauty in the world despite hardships.

Chad Hugo, Shay Haley, and Pharrell Williams (*left to right*) created N.E.R.D. with the purpose of expanding their musical tastes and abilities.

CHAPTER 3
PHARRELL GOES SOLO

Pharrell's first solo album was called *In My Mind*. Released in 2005, Pharrell worked with big names such as Gwen Stefani, Kanye West, and Daddy Yankee for the album. The album rose to #3 on the charts and sold 142,000 copies in its first week!

PRODUCING, COMPOSING, COLLABORATING

While still working with both the Neptunes and N.E.R.D., Pharrell took on some producing jobs on his own. He worked with Beyonce, Britney Spears, and the Hives.

Pharrell has worked with many diverse artists, inlcuding Gwen Stefani and Kanye West.

In 2008, he worked with the legendary Madonna. He also worked with Shakira, Jennifer Lopez, and rapper the Game. He was building a name for himself and showing that he had an ear for music that stretched over all genres of music.

In 2010, Pharrell composed the sound track to the biggest animated movie of the year, *Despicable Me.* This project helped to push Pharrell into using his musical talents in different parts of the entertainment industry.

Soon after, Pharrell worked with Hans Zimmer to compose and produce the music for the 84th Academy Awards. It seemed that if it had to do with music, Pharrell was involved. But he was about to get even bigger.

"HAPPY"

In 2013, Pharrell experienced his biggest success to date. He was brought on to work on the music for *Despicable Me 2.*

The Minions became the most popular characters from *Despicable Me*.

He wrote and produced the smash-hit "Happy." The song was also the lead single for Pharrell's second solo studio album, called *Girl*.

The song was #1 in the United States, the United Kingdom, Canada, Ireland, New Zealand, and nineteen other

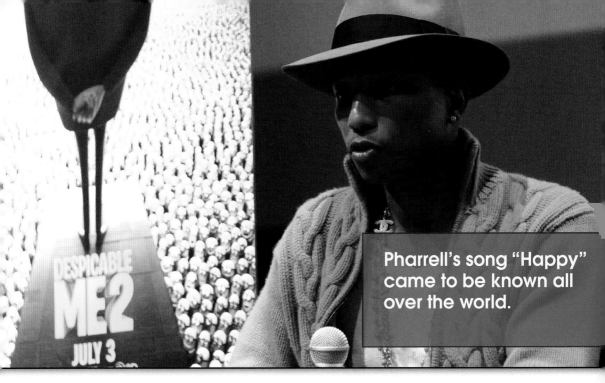

Pharrell's song "Happy" came to be known all over the world.

countries. It was nominated for an Academy Award for "Best Original Song" and won a Grammy Award for "Best Pop Solo Performance" at the 57th Grammy Awards. It also won a Grammy for "Best Music Video."

People from all over the globe made their own music videos dancing to the song. It was a cultural phenomenon that brought people together and promoted happiness in the face of adversity. "Happy" became the most successful song of 2014.

CHAPTER 4
A N.E.R.D. OF MANY HATS

Through all his success as a musician and producer, first and foremost, Pharrell is a family man. On October 12, 2013, Pharrell married his long-time girlfriend, model and designer Helen Lasichanh, in France. Together they have a son named Rocket Williams, who was born in November 2008.

In 2008, Pharrell founded the charity From One Hand to AnOTHER (FOHTA). Pharrell believes that

In 2014, Pharrell received a star on the Hollywood Walk of Fame. His family attended the event with him.

every child can be a success if only he or she has the right education, experience, and tools. His organization is fighting to provide every child with an equal opportunity to be successful in society. For the past ten years, FOHTA has donated supplies to classrooms in need. He also gave back to his hometown by offering free after-school and summer innovation camps to children in the Virginia Beach and Hampton Bay areas.

FASHION DESIGNER AND ICON

Adding to his resume in 2005, Pharrell created the clothing brands Billionaire Boys Club and Ice Cream footwear. He helped design everything from T-shirts to suits and outerwear.

He helped design a line of jewelry as well as eyeglasses for Louis Vuitton in 2008 and Moncler in 2013. He also worked closely with Adidas and G-Star Raw.

Pharrell Says:

"[I'm] committed to bringing kids experiences that ignite their passions, challenge their minds, and prepare them for success."

Pharrell received all these opportunities due to his own unique style. He was often seen walking the red carpet in odd hats, suit jackets with shorts, and his Adidas sneakers. Because of his major influence on the fashion world, he was honored as a CFDA Fashion Icon.

Fun Fact
For every $1,000 in music sold, the average musician makes $23.40.

THE VOICE

In 2014, Pharrell became a new coach for *The Voice*. The show chooses talented people based solely on their voices. If the **contestant's** voice made an impact, a celebrity coach would turn his or her chair around and hope to coach the artist. It sent a message to the public that the most important aspect of music is talent, not looks.

The contestants also got to choose whom they wanted to coach them. Each coach would build a team of singers that competed against each other for the final prize. In the eighth season, Pharrell's artist, sixteen-year-old Sawyer Fredericks, won the competition.

Pharrell Says:
"I love the world."

Pharrell loved the opportunity to give back to the community of artists. He was the perfect coach since he has worked with such a diverse group of artists in his career and has an ear for all genres of music. It showcased him as not only a master of his craft, but also as someone to look up to for advice and encouragement.

This outfit, worn to the 2014 Grammys, became iconic for Pharrell.

AUTHOR

Pharrell signed a book deal with Putnam Books for Young Readers to write four children's books. The first book was named after his biggest hit. *Happy* depicts children all over the world revealing what it means to be happy.

The book is a way for Pharrell to communicate the importance of remembering moments of happiness and that by being positive, children can make their future brighter.

TIMELINE

1973 Pharrell Williams is born on April 5 in Virginia Beach, Virginia.

1992 Teddy Riley discovers the Neptunes.

1999 N.E.R.D. is formed.

2001 First interantional hit, Britney Spears's "I'm a Slave 4 U."

2003 Neptunes' first album, *The Neptunes Present…Clones,* is released.

2004 The Neptunes win two Grammy Awards.

2005 Pharrell Williams creates Billionaire Boys Club and Ice Cream footwear.

2005 Pharrell releases first solo album, *In My Mind.*

2008 Rocket Williams is born.

2008 Pharrell founds his charity From One Hand to AnOTHER.

2010 Pharrell helps compose sound track for *Despicable Me.*

2011 Pharrell helps compose music for the 84th Academy Awards.

2013 Pharrell Williams marries Helen Lasichanh on October 12.

2014 Pharrell's song "Happy" is a smash hit.

2014 Pharrell becomes a coach on *The Voice.*

2015 Pharrell's artist Sawyer Fredericks wins *The Voice.*

2015 *Happy* is published as a book for children.

LEARN MORE

BOOKS

Burling, Alexis. *Pharrell Williams: Grammy-Winning Singer, Songwriter & Producer.* Edina, MN: ABDO Publishing Company, 2015.

Morreale, Marie. *Pharrell Williams.* New York, NY: Scholastic Library Publishing, 2015.

Williams, Pharrell. *Happy.* New York, NY: Penguin Young Readers Group, 2015.

WEBSITES

From One Hand to AnOTHER

fohta.org

Learn about Pharrell's charity, which is a nonprofit organization that provides school supplies to classrooms in need.

Compose Your Very Own Music!

www.classicsforkids.com/games/compose/compose.html

This interactive game lets you make your own music by dragging notes onto the staff.

Index

Published in 2017 by Enslow Publishing, LLC.
101 W. 23rd Street, Suite 240, New York, NY 10011

Library of Congress Cataloging-in-Publication Data:
Names: Flores, Christopher Lee, author.
Title: Pharrell Williams: singer and songwriter / Christopher Lee Flores.
Description: New York : Enslow Publishing, 2017. | Series: Junior biographies |
Includes bibliographical references and index.
Identifiers: LCCN 2016020288| ISBN 9780766081949 (library bound) | ISBN
9780766081925 (pbk.) | ISBN 9780766081932 (6-pack)
Subjects: LCSH: Williams, Pharrell—Juvenile literature. | Rap musicians—United
States—Biography—Juvenile literature. | Singers—United States—Biography—
Juvenile literature.
Classification: LCC ML3930.W55 F56 2016 | DDC 782.421649092 [B] —dc23
LC record available at https://lccn.loc.gov/2016020288

Printed in China

Photo Credits: Cover, p. 1 Mireya Acierto/Getty Images; p. 4 Helga Esteb/
Shutterstock.com; p. 6 Ritu Manoj Jethani/Shutterstock.com; p. 7 J. Shearer/
WireImage/Getty Images; p. 9 Gabriel Olsen/FilmMagic/Getty Images; p. 10 Scott
Gries/Getty Images; p. 13 Paul Natkin/WireImage/Getty Images; p. 14 Chris Polk/
FilmMagic/Getty Images; p. 16 Photos 12/Alamy Stock Photo; p. 17 David Buchan/
Getty Images; p. 18 Chelsea Lauren/WireImage/Getty Images; p. 21 Robyn Beck/
AFP/Getty Images; back cover and interior pages graphics Alena Kazlouskaya/
Shutterstock.com.